Face To Face, Based Pointer Of Linked List Called Collaboration

A Proposal To Reshape International Collaboration

Edward Seymour

Face To Face, Based Pointer Of Linked List Called Collaboration

A Proposal To Reshape International Collaboration

Edward Seymour

This text is dedicated to suggesting a revised model for
international collaboration with vastly increased efficacy

Table of Contents

About the author

I began my study of commerce with a master known as Ed Talbot under an operation called a 5 and Dime store while attending high school. I inadvertently absorbed much of his views on equitable commerce with an emphasis on directed charity. This was also a study in the value of delegation, loss accounting, forecasting and the time value of money.

Deming

In college I was introduced to Deming
http://www.economist.com/node/13805735 A synopsis of his
philosophy was following:

simplicity trumps complexity every time

Look around Shanghai, on foot, slowly, with attention to detail.

Elegant == Simple

Simple, Repeatable == Quality

Next, two years out of college, I was appointed as an IBM manager and sent to Corporate Management School. Principals emphasized therein were mind blowing.

Perception==Reality.

Regardless of your own image of fact, or truth, it is immaterial if others perception differs. From IBM management school I learned "tell them, tell them what you told them, Ask them what they heard". Many lack the patience and follow through to complete all steps..

Customer Is ALWAYS right!

Just like when you go to a store to buy something, you have definite needs. Anyone who ignores your requests will not get your business. While it is disrespectful to deny a need exists, there is an option to advise on an alternative solution as long as it addresses the expressed need. Arrogance is simply pretense.

Think

It is, simply put, my opinion that there is enormous benefit in cross cultural collaboration. It has implicit benefits of covering the globe 24x7. It can also make 1+1==19. It, however requires adherence to simply policies to enable. Several of the underlying concepts are covered in my text called

Zen And The Art Of Teaching

In summary, regardless of the collaboration model, It will benefit from this new view. It could be

Customer/Supplier, Vendor/Customer or Company/Company Elsewhere

Any effectiveness is derived from mutual trust. Trust does not arise from feeling superior or being arrogant. Along those lines, those who perceive themselves less worthy as a result of an interaction will lack trust.

Elegance and Simplicity are Co Requisites

No one will buy a high end luxury vehicle which takes a trained master to operate. The essence of luxury is "how could something so great, be so simple."

Secrets Are To Be Shared Among Friends In A Brief Whisper

Unless you can express something succinctly, it fails to exist in perception. Thus, I propose no more than 2-3 pages, liberally illustrated to convey any astounding new method, technique or product.

Face To Face IS ABSOLUTELY NEEDED At First

Initially this will consist of sharing culture, food traditions and stories. This provides the walking path to mutual trust.

Background

This text represents about 36 years of experience with customers, international collaborations and intellectual discourse. In this period I have gained a clue as to effective and conversely annoying arrangements. While there is a time and place for both, I suggest a prescription for effectiveness that relies simply on building trust, defending honor and keeping perception in check.

Ideas herein are mine.

Albeit, my views are reshaped daily by interaction.

Thus, one could say this is a study of accumulated knowledge with sources too numerous to recount..

Crux Of My Idea

Picture is worth a thousand words, use them wisely.

Caption is essence of picture.

Food Seems To Be Essence of Culture.

Language is something to study and use.

At the end of the day "When in Rome, Do As The Romans Do"

*To understand something incredibly complex,
describe the essence.*

Essence can be sight, smell, touch, feel, but is always conveyed instantaneously

KISS principle (Keep It Simple Stupid)

Never derive that which is commonly understood

Never convey without comprehension.

www.ingramcontent.com/pod-product-compliance
Lightning Source LLC
Chambersburg PA
CBHW021855170526
45157CB00006B/2454